RISE UP
FOR YOU

TRANSFORM YOUR TEAM AND O

Where People Come First

We help organizations transform their workplace culture, wellbeing and expand their leadership through soft skills development.

About

Rise Up For You works with clients around the world to enhance company leadership, growth, and overall development through transformational coaching, training, on-demand learning, and educational events.

Our mission is to elevate you, your organizations and your team's potential by providing high-quality training and coaching in soft skills– the most needed skills today and in the future. Make our superpower your superpower! Elevate your leadership, emotional intelligence, communication, confidence, success, and more.

Rise Up For You has global reach in North America, MENA, and Europe

Our Impact Theory

Empower and **enhance transformational leadership** for the greater good of the organization, team, and overall vision.

Support the **next generation of competent and competitive individuals** to enter the workforce.

Soft Skills and EQ Impact Theory

Prepare, reflect, and **counter balance the use and rapid evolution of AI.** Where people come first!

Stronger Communities | Thriving Economy | High Performing Work Culture | Greater Collaboration | Happy Homes

Where People Come First

RISE UP
FOR YOU

 # Our Values

Integrity

Staying true to our values, morals, and ethics. Rise Up For You will always maintain the highest integrity and takes pride in maintaining the highest principles both professionally and personally.

Quality

We hold ourselves to rigorous standards, ensuring that every aspect of what we offer reflects precision, authenticity, and effectiveness. From our educational content and training programs to our interactions with individuals, quality is the measure by which we gauge success.

Ownership

Ownership is the embodiment of responsibility and accountability at Rise Up For You. It signifies the proactive embrace of challenges, the willingness to learn from mistakes, and the commitment to driving positive change. We take ownership and empower others to take ownership.

Solution Oriented

Being solution-focused places a strong emphasis on positivity, client-centeredness, and future orientation. It strives to uncover existing solutions and resources, respecting individuals' autonomy and preferences while fostering collaboration and empowerment.

Transformational

Transformational leaders value trust, collaboration, and continuous learning, creating a positive and forward-thinking culture that catalyzes significant and lasting transformations in individuals and organizations. Our transformational approach lies in its ability to drive meaningful and sustainable change, unlocking untapped potential and achieving exceptional results.

Why Rise Up For You?

Expertise and Experience:
Rise Up For You has a team of experienced professionals who are well-versed in various areas, including leadership development, communication skills, diversity and inclusion, and career advancement. Each team member holds credentials, post-baccalaureate degrees, and various certifications in the appropriate fields related to soft skills, leadership and organizational development.

Strategic and Sustainable Approach:
We constantly evaluate our goals, aligning them with emerging opportunities, and ensuring that every action propels us towards long-term success with you and your team. Our strategic and sustainable approach is not just ideals of "hype" but tangible steps integrated into our everyday actions.

Empowering and Neutral Methods:
We believe in fostering an environment where individuals are empowered to reach their full potential, irrespective of background or position. Our commitment to neutrality ensures fairness and equity in all interactions, promoting a culture that values diversity, inclusivity, and equitable opportunities.

Credible Content and Certification: Rise Up For You is proudly certified through SHRM (Society for Human Resources Management). All content and programming has gone through a rigorous curriculum check to ensure high quality content and education Is being delivered on a continuous basis. Every piece of content and certification issued by our organization is a testament to our unwavering dedication to quality and trustworthiness.

Measured Results and Assessments:
We implement rigorous measurement processes and assessments across our endeavors. This commitment to measurement allows us to adapt, evolve, and excel, fostering a culture of continuous improvement where data-driven insights guide our path to sustainable success.

Transformative Training Programs

- Leveling Up Inside Out: A Deep Dive into Emotional Intelligence
- Rising Leadership: Igniting Change and Inspiring Others
- EmpowerHer: A Blueprint for Women in Leadership
- Mindset Mastery: A Guide to Personal Growth and Success
- Executive Charisma: Public Speaking for Leadership Impact
- Career Confidence 101: Strategies for Success in the Workplace

***Program Mix and Mingle Customization Is available*

Training Program
Base Deliverables

*** *Training programs and partnerships are long form, immersive, and strategic in development for long term success.*

Core Training

- Culture, training, and organizational needs analysis
- Emotional Intelligence 360 assessments for the team
- Monthly consultation and coaching for the lead contact
- Curated and customized content developed based on the client objectives
- Diverse teaching methods that are experiential and stimulating
- Strategic Handbook 168 pages for each participant
- A team of Rise Up For You Trainers handpicked for your team
- Post training reports, assessments, recommendations for program sustainability

Success Membership- 1yr

- 100+ videos and workbooks, Topics Include Public speaking, Career Confidence, Leadership, Time Management and more.
- Curriculum Handbook downloadable for each course plus additional downloadable resources added each quarter.
- LIVE Trainings every month with our global community
  - Each month the Rise Up For You team will go live for members only sharing new content and allowing for Q and A.
- Certificate of Completion once core courses are complete: 36 SHRM PDC's
- Pre and post assessments for your team on Emotional Intelligence, Confidence, and Whole Success
- 1 free coaching session for each team member
- Administrative access to monitor team progress

Accountability Toolbox- 1yr

- Leadership Circle Check-ins every second Monday
- Done for you scripts
  - Program roll out templates
  - LIVE reminder templates
  - Monthly motivation templates for each month
- Accountability Activities e-Book
- Culture Roadmap e-Book
- Performance Review templates
- Motivational Interviewing questions for hiring

Training Program
General Timeline

Phase 1- Contact and Decision Makers

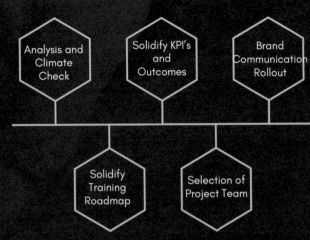

- Analysis and Climate Check
- Solidify KPI's and Outcomes
- Brand Communication Rollout
- Solidify Training Roadmap
- Selection of Project Team

Phase 2- Participants Training Development

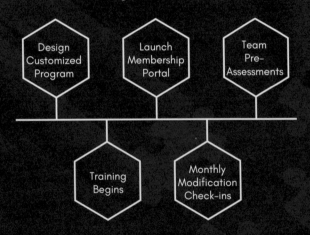

- Design Customized Program
- Launch Membership Portal
- Team Pre-Assessments
- Training Begins
- Monthly Modification Check-ins

Phase 3- Contact and Decision Makers

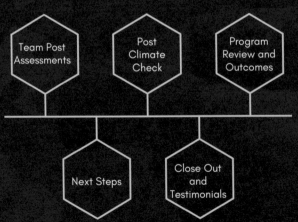

- Team Post Assessments
- Post Climate Check
- Program Review and Outcomes
- Next Steps
- Close Out and Testimonials

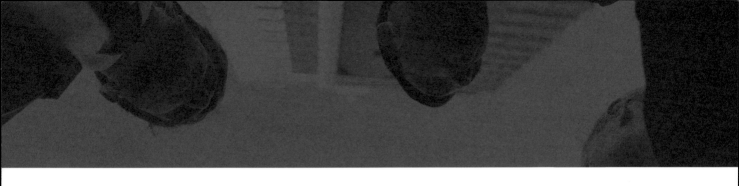

Additional Ala Carte Services

- 1-1 Coaching
- Ala Carte Development
- Rise Global Success Membership

Coach with Us

Executive Coaching- *$6999 USD*

Executive coaching is a ***highly personalized and intensive development program that is designed to help senior leaders enhance their skills and performance.*** The program is typically conducted in a one-on-one setting and is tailored to the individual needs and goals of the executive.

The coach works closely with the executive to help them identify and overcome any obstacles that may be hindering their performance. This may include developing strategies to improve communication, decision-making, conflict resolution, and other key leadership competencies.

Employee Coaching- *$4999 USD*

Team and 1-1 leadership coaching is a service designed to support individuals and teams in developing their leadership and soft skills to enhance their performance. This service involves working with an experienced coach who provides guidance and support to help individuals and teams achieve their goals.

1-1 coaching is focused on the development of individual leaders. The coach works closely with the leader to identify areas for improvement, set goals, and develop strategies to enhance their leadership skills. This may include improving communication, decision-making, conflict resolution, and other key leadership competencies.

Coaching Features

- 12 sessions 1-1 for optimal growth and customization
- RISE assessments to measure your growth in EQ, Employee Confidence and Success
- Full access to the RISE Global Success Membership for 1 yr

 Available virtually 12-30 minutes sessions to be used between 3-6 months

Ala Carte Development
— 90 mins $3,999, Half Day $7,999 Full Day $13,999 USD

Ala Carte workshops and training retreats are customized programs designed specifically for your team to help them develop new skills, improve collaboration, and enhance overall performance. These programs offer a range of flexible options to choose from, allowing you to tailor the experience to your team's specific needs.

Workshops are typically short-term programs that focus on a specific skill or topic, such as communication, leadership, or conflict resolution. These sessions can range from a few hours to several days and can be delivered in-person or virtually.

The training retreats, on the other hand, are more immersive experiences that typically ***take place over a half to several days.*** These retreats are designed to allow your team to step away from their everyday work environment and focus solely on the development of new skills, building relationships, and enhancing teamwork.

Overall, Ala Carte workshops and training retreats are an excellent way to invest in the growth and development of your team while getting to know the training and methods of Rise Up For You.

Ala Carte Features

- Training Needs Analysis
- Customized Programming
- Workshop-Style delivery
- Multilingual Trainers
- Resources Provided

 Available virtually or In person

Rise Global Membership- *$299 USD per user*
Have more than 500 employees?
Ask us about our 500+ membership discount

Our membership is your passport to unlocking the intangible powerhouses that define true success – the soft skills.

As a member, you'll have exclusive access to expert-led masterclasses, personalized coaching sessions, and a treasure trove of resources designed to elevate your soft skills game. Whether you're a seasoned professional looking to refine your edge or a budding talent hungry for knowledge, we've crafted an ecosystem where everyone thrives.

Join us, not just to succeed, but to thrive in a world that demands more than just technical know-how. Soft Skills for Success is not just a membership; it's your catalyst for a career and life that transcends expectations. Embrace the power of the intangible, and let success become your second nature.

Membership Features:

- 100+ videos and workbooks, Topics Include Public speaking, Career Confidence, Leadership, Time Management and more.
- Curriculum Handbook downloadable for each course plus additional downloadable resources added each quarter.
- LIVE Trainings every month with our global community
  - Each month the Rise Up For You team will go live for members only sharing new content and allowing for Q and A.
- Certificate of Completion once core courses are complete: 36 SHRM PDC's
- Pre and post assessments for your team on Emotional Intelligence, Confidence, and Whole Success
- 1 free coaching session for each participant

 Available virtually   At your own pace, 1 yr

Featured On

SHRM RECERTIFICATION PROVIDER

Rise Up For You is proudly recognized by SHRM to offer Professional Development Credits (PDCs) for the SHRM-CP® or SHRM-SCP®. All trainings, courses, and coaching programs are fully accredited by SHRM and do provide PDC'S to you and your team.

WOMEN OWNED
CERTIFIED BY | WOMEN'S BUSINESS ENTERPRISE NATIONAL COUNCIL

Officially Women Owned Certified Business: Rise Up For You is proudly certified through WBENC the largest third-party certifier of businesses owned, controlled, and operated by women in the United States.

Bloomberg Television

CBC ◉ Radio-Canada

 tv+

◉ CBS

Entrepreneur

Global EDMONTON

Just a Few of Our Clients

Our Team In Action

Contact Us

Follow Us @riseupforyou

 riseupforyou.com

USA Headquarters
Las Vegas, Nevada 89129
702-268-9997
info@riseupforyou.com
NLN@riseupforyou.com

Canadian Region
Edmonton, Alberta
780-905-5455
mona@riseupforyou.com

United Arab Emirates Headquarters
Dubai, United Arab Emirates
nnasserdeen@riseupforyou.com

Maximizing Your Potential for an Extraordinary Life

Elevating Your Confidence and Success

Where People Come First

 nln@riseupforyou.com   📞 949-229-0208   🌐 www.riseupforyou.com

Preface

Welcome to this strategic workbook on personal and leadership development! This workbook is designed to help you enhance your personal growth and develop your leadership skills. The purpose of this workbook is to provide you with practical tools and exercises that you can use to become a more effective leader, both in your personal and professional life.

Personal development is the process of improving yourself, your knowledge, your skills, your habits, your beliefs, and your values. It involves self-awareness, self-reflection, and self-improvement. Leadership, on the other hand, is the process of inspiring, motivating, and influencing others to achieve a common goal. It involves the ability to communicate effectively, make decisions, solve problems, delegate tasks, and build relationships.

The first section of the book starts with self-awareness, which is the foundation of personal growth and leadership. It includes exercises and tools to help you identify your strengths, weaknesses, values, and beliefs. We will go through goal-setting, which is critical for achieving success in any area of life. Tools to help you set specific, measurable, achievable, relevant, and time-bound goals will be provided to support your growth.

The 6 Pillars to Success

It's important to know that culture and community play a part in how we define "success." In North America we have fallen into a vicious cycle of hustle culture just to survive!

It can feel like a never-ending cycle to work all day to gain healthcare benefits, to pay off student debt, to eventually live a free life while in the meantime you're stressed about family time, playing with your kids, and trying to take care of your own health. For many, by the time they feel a sense of freedom, they have already mismanaged their health, missed out on parenting opportunities, and/or are potentially moving toward a divorce or going through multiple heartbreaks due to ignoring their relationships.

The main thing to understand here as a leader and influencer, is that these circumstances impact people and their behaviors. When individuals feel stuck, overwhelmed with debt, weighed down by life decisions, it impacts their ability to show up as their best which means it impacts their communication, emotional management, ability to lead others, and motivation on a daily basis. In fact, this is also true for us as leaders as we are also going through similar challenges that directly impact our presence, energy, and communication.

Your time is now to create your success and get to the next level as a leader but first we must understand where we are today as a WHOLE PERSON and how it impacts how we show up with others.

Research shows that the happiest, most fulfilled people in the world are the ones who make time to nurture and build their Relationships with People, Money, Self-Worth, Career, Romance, Health and Fitness. When we feel great inside, as the whole person, then and only then can we create positive change around us.

The data from Gallup's World Happiness Report shows that between 2009 and 2017, well-being and happiness among Americans actually declined in all 50 states. Although salary and other economic factors play important roles, once basic needs are met, a person's sense of well-being is mostly determined by positive relationships, engagement, health, and a personal sense of meaning, purpose, and accomplishment.

The 6 Pillars to Mastering Success

When your focus on one pillar suffers, it has a negative effect on the rest. Focusing on the WHOLE person is a forgotten practice in today's world. We are bringing it back so that all men and women can live their best lives while empowering others to do the same.

Let's work together to provide you with an action plan that can make you feel more secure and happy in life. It's time to rise up to the next level and become your best self!

Again, when we feel great inside, as the whole person, then and only then; can we create positive change around us.

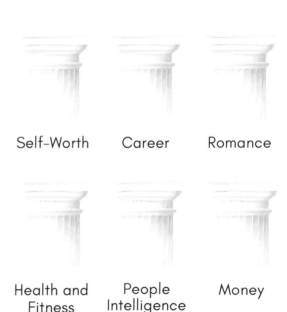

Self-Worth   Career   Romance

Health and   People   Money
Fitness   Intelligence

The 6 Pillars to Mastering Success

When we examine the elements that affect us and our well-being the most, we can break it down to these six areas:

Self-Worth

If you remember anything from this book, remember this: self-actualization and self-worth are the key to sustainable success. Your potential and your ability to grow and build a life that you are proud of is fully dependent on how you feel and what you think about yourself. Your thoughts and beliefs about yourself drive your actions, motivations, and the ability to make decisions which are in alignment with your true authentic self.

Career

In its State Of The Global Workplace report for 2022, Gallup states that "85% of employees are not actively engaged or (are) actively disengaged at work." Raising it 15% from pre-pandemic workplace statistics. This means that only 15% of employees are actively engaged. This has been one of the key factors for the rise in entrepreneurs, coaches, consultants, and small online start-ups. People today want more than a paycheck and the COVID pandemic escalated the entrepreneur mindset and lifestyle. The modern day workforce wants meaning, growth, development, positive leadership, and most importantly, a trajectory for their career laid out.

People are hungry to make an impact and are seeking something more in life. The main question here is: what do you want in your career, why do you want it, and what is it going to take to get there if you're not there already?

The 6 Pillars to Mastering Success

RISEUP
FOR YOU

Romance

This pillar matters because it affects us mentally, physically, and emotionally, on a level that is inexplicable. Nights where you can't sleep because you got into an argument, the deep pit in your stomach when you have a break-up, yet you still need to show up at work with your best foot forward. Lonely nights that make you question if you're really worthy of someone else's love. We've all been there and we've all felt the effects.

What do you want in a partner and what are the non-negotiables? Ask yourself and those close to you who have a strong relationship if your non-negotiables are realistic or filled with expectations that go beyond our control.

Health and Fitness

Does it make sense to you that we spend our whole life building our wealth to then turn it around and spend it on our health? We fall into this trap of external praise and materialistic glory and forget how important it is to nurture our physical, nutritional, and mental health. YES! All three of them matter.

Today we have the highest suicide and depression rates while the cases of cardiac disease and cancer continue to increase, and more and more people are losing their health and ability to enjoy life in their body and mind.

Don't wait until it's too late.

The 6 Pillars to Mastering Success

Relationship Intelligence

This pillar's specific focus is on communication, leadership skills, and soft skills—such as emotional and social intelligence, conflict resolution, and networking strategies. This does not include your romantic life as we have classified that as a separate pillar.

Individuals are affected and influenced by those who surround them. Building professional and personal relationships is a crucial part of your happiness and success. You may be familiar with the famous quote from Jim Rohn: "You are the average of the five people you spend the most time with." Shilagh Mirgain, Ph.D UW Health Psychologist echoes this famous sentiment as she explains that "happiness isn't just a personal experience, it is actually affected by the individuals around you." Mirgain continues:

Money

According to a new survey by Ramsey Solutions, "money fights are the second-leading cause of divorce, behind infidelity. Results show that both high levels of debt and a lack of communication are major causes for the stress and anxiety surrounding household finances."

Understanding how to make money work for you is crucial in formulating a financial plan. This pillar is specific to financial literacy, money management, budgeting, investing, and spending habits and beliefs.

Start Up Exercise

Rise Up For You encourages CONTINUOUS GROWTH in becoming your best self. This means that no matter where you are in your life, challenge yourself to rise even higher!

Let's take a moment and assess where you are in each pillar of life currently. Follow the 6 Pillars to Success Self-Assessment on the next page and let's begin the journey to become your best.

Rate the 6 pillars between 1-10 (see next page)

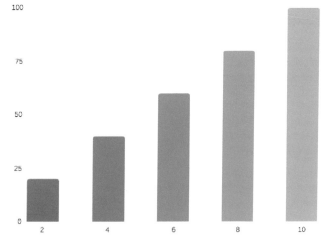

1-2= Needs a lot of work and is far from my goal. I am not happy with this at all!

3-4= It's existent but not consistent. I'm not happy with this.

5-6= Needs improvement but I am half way there. More hard work and I'll achieve my level of happiness in this pillar.

7-8= I am happy with this pillar! I'm really close to exactly what I want and I feel pretty great about it.

9-10= I feel great! This pillar is in alignment with me and I feel that I am currently at my best!

Step #1

This is a great visual indicator to address which areas need more love and nurturing. Rate each pillar 1-10, 10 being your optimal thriving zone and 1 being your danger zone. How off balance is your circle? For your lowest pillar, what is one thing you can do to get to your next level in the next month?

Danger Zone- Level 1

Thriving Zone- Level 10

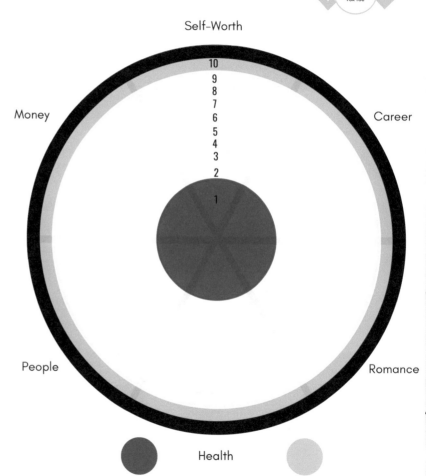

Step #2

Now that you have evaluated each element, let's develop specific goals and outline a plan to achieve them. What small, actionable steps can you take now to rise to the next level? Start small so you don't overwhelm yourself. Perhaps you can start by saving 10% of your monthly income to invest in future property, working out for 10- minutes twice a week if you haven't exercised in a while, or working 30-minutes every night to start formulating that start-up business idea you have always dreamed about! Create your action plan below by listing one step you can take to start achieving your new goals.

Self-Worth

Career

Romance

Health

People

Money

My take away from the 6 Pillars of Success is:

_____

_____

_____

_____

_____

_____

SCAN THE QR CODE TO ACCESS YOUR FREE COURSE ON
HOW TO MASTER SUCCESS IN ALL AREAS OF YOUR LIFE!

Notes

Building Confidence In Your Career and Life

Building Confidence

Even today, there is a particular crisis when it comes to confidence both professionally and personally. Professionals around the world have expressed their frustrations and struggles as they attempt to climb the career ladder or achieve next-level results in their personal and professional lives. Our research indicates that 83% of working professionals struggle with confidence in the workplace.

With years of coaching individuals on career confidence and leadership strategies, the Rise Up For You Team has recognized the top four challenges for professionals.

Imposter Syndrome- Not feeling good enough or afraid that you don't bring enough value to the table.

Self-Promotion- Struggling with the idea of advocating for and asserting yourself when needed for work promotions, networking, and new opportunities.

Climbing the Career Ladder- Feeling unsure how to climb the ladder and get to the next step in your career often includes feelings of being unseen and unheard.

Taking Risk- Finding it difficult to take risks at appropriate times, potentially missing out on advances for you and your career.

The great news is confidence can be developed through proven science-based strategies, which means that we can close the confidence gap, especially among underrepresented communities in the workforce.

Building Confidence

Confidence is already in you, and it's stronger and more needed than you think. Everyone needs confidence and we all struggle from a lack of it in one way or another. You can be confident in a particular skill, but you can also be confident in some areas of your life and less in others. For example, you may be reading this thinking: "I am incredibly confident in my career and professional relationships." You're successful, move up the career ladder, and have no problem speaking up in a professional environment. But perhaps you are lacking confidence in your love life. Perhaps you haven't met the right partner and over time that has made you feel unloveable, messing with your confidence to connect with a romantic partner. This is what I like to call **Macro- and Micro-confidence.**

- **Micro-confidence:** *a belief in yourself as it relates to one particular area, skill or competency. You are a confident singer, or perhaps confident in your job role. This level of confidence is not sustainable and is constantly shifting.*
- **Macro-confidence:** *a deep rooted belief in oneself that you can and will overcome, achieve and make the proper decisions for yourself and your future success. This level of confidence is sustainable and transferable in any job, relationship, life experience, etc. The Macro level gives you the confidence and belief to build more micro confidence. For example, learning a new skill, being adaptable, making the ask.*

It's important to cultivate the Macro level of confidence for sustainable success and fulfillment. Micro-confidence is not sustainable. It's the extra cherry on top once you have cultivated confidence on the macro level.

Macro vs Micro

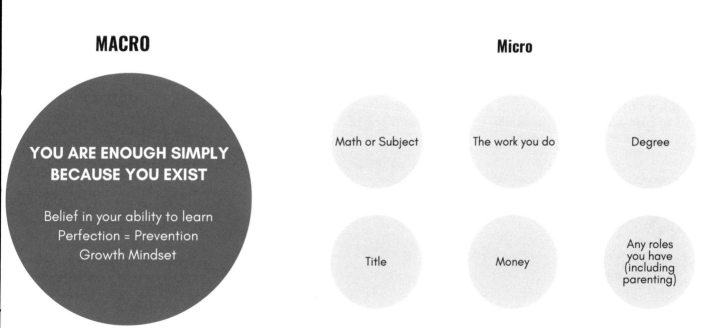

MACRO

YOU ARE ENOUGH SIMPLY BECAUSE YOU EXIST

Belief in your ability to learn
Perfection = Prevention
Growth Mindset

Micro

Math or Subject

The work you do

Degree

Title

Money

Any roles you have (including parenting)

Confidence Quiz

SCAN THE QR CODE BELOW TO ASSESS YOUR CONFIDENCE!

On a scale of 1-10, 10 being your optimal thriving zone and 1 being your danger zone, rate yourself in each pillar. Add up your total score and divide by 60 to get your percentage. Be sure to keep track of your score along the way!

How did you score on the confidence assessment? Which competency did you want to focus on and how will you get there?

Self Talk _____

Trusting Intuition _____

Taking Risk _____

Self Promotion _____

Setting Boundaries _____

Growth Mindset _____

Exercise Time:
The 4 B's to Believing
In You!

Write down a fear, belief, or doubt that is hindering your success.

Step 1: Write down a fear, belief, or doubt that is hindering your success.

Step 2: Write down the backstory or your past experience that is associated with this fear or belief. Try to be as specific as possible. Trace your belief back to one moment, experience, or situation.

Step 3: Write down the behavior the belief is causing. For example, is it causing you to play small? To keep quiet in meetings? To be aggressive unnecessarily?

Step 4: Ask yourself, "How can I break the belief to shift the behavior?" Do you still want the backstory (person or experience) to have power over you? How do we take your power back once and for all?

Repeat this exercise for each limiting belief that pops up.

THE BELIEF- The limiting belief getting in your way

THE BACKSTORY- where it comes from

THE BEHAVIOR- what behaviors occur

THE BREAKING- how do we move past this belief?

RISE UP
FOR YOU

"The greatest tragedy today is wasted human potential."

SCAN THE QR CODE NOW TO ACCESS A FREE COURSE ON
HOW TO REGAIN CONFIDENCE AND CLARITY IN YOUR CAREER AND LIFE!

Additional Resources

Grab It Here

The Rise Success Journal

With the Success Journal, you'll be able to set clear and achievable goals, break them down into actionable steps, and track your progress towards success. Our carefully crafted prompts and exercises will guide you through self-reflection, mindset shifts and gratitude practices to help you cultivate a positive and growth-oriented mindset.

Grab It Here

Rise Up For You- Closing the Gap Between You and Your Potential

The time is now to create your success and get to the next level that is in alignment with your life and heart. "Nada states, "The greatest tragedy is wasted human potential."In this inspiring and empowering book, Nada draws from both her personal life-changing experiences and professional experiences as a past international performer, executive, educator, and now entrepreneur to show how we can close the gap between ourselves and our untapped potential.

Join Our Membership

Ready to push yourself to the next level? Take advantage of our membership below and get $100 off!

When you join our global annual membership you get to:

- Gain exclusive access to LIVE trainings for members only, every month with our training team.
- Access to hundreds of on-demand videos to transform any area of your life on:
  - Confidence
  - Public Speaking
  - Becoming a Coach
  - Emotional Intelligence
  - And more!
- Unlock new content and videos added each month
- Receive 1 FREE VIP Coaching Session

Enroll here

Join today for one low annual payment! Scan the code below or go here: programs.riseupforyou.com/product/growthmembership

USE CODE: SPECIAL100 for your $100 discount

Redeem within 30 days

Get 15% off all training and development

$1000 off any coaching program

Contact Us

 NLN@riseupforyou.com or
Team@riseupforyou.com

 949-229-0208

 @riseupforyou

 www.riseupforyou.com

Made in the USA
Columbia, SC
12 August 2024

39992131R00024